The Ideal Bartender

by Tom Bullock

Originally published in 1917.

DEDICATED

TO THOSE WHO ENJOY SNUG CLUB ROOMS, THAT
THEY MAY LEARN THE ART OF PREPARING FOR
THEMSELVES WHAT IS GOOD.

IS IT ANY WONDER THAT MANKIND STANDS
OPEN-MOUTHED BEFORE THE BARTENDER,
CONSIDERING THE MYSTERIES AND MARVELS OF
AN ART THAT BORDERS ON MAGIC? RECIPES
FOUND IN THIS BOOK HAVE BEEN COMPOSED
AND COLLECTED, TRIED AND TESTED, IN A
QUARTER-CENTURY OF EXPERIENCE BY TOM
BULLOCK OF THE ST. LOUIS COUNTRY CLUB.

A testimonial from the St. Louis Post-Dispatch which appeared in the form of an editorial, Wednesday evening, May 28, 1913, at a time when Col. Roosevelt was vindicating, by a libel suit, his reputation for sobriety and temperance.

Colonel Roosevelt's fatal admission that he drank just a part of one julep at the St. Louis Country Club will come very near losing his case.

Who was ever known to drink just a part of one of Tom's? Tom, than whom there is no greater mixologist of any race, color or condition of servitude, was taught the art of the julep by no less than Marse Lilburn G. McNair, the father of the julep. In fact, the very cup that Col. Roosevelt drank it from belonged to Governor McNair, the first Governor of Missouri, the great-grandfather of Marse Lilburn and the great-great-grandfather of the julep.

As is well known, the Country Club mint originally sprang on the slopes of Parnassus and was transplanted thence to the bosky banks of Culpeper Creek, Gaines County, Ky., and thence to our own environs; while the classic distillation with which Tom mingles it to produce his chief d'oeuvre is the oft-quoted liquefied soul of a Southern moonbeam falling aslant the dewy slopes of the Cumberland Mountains.

To believe that a red-blooded man, and a true Colonel at that, ever stopped with just a part of one of those refreshments which have made St. Louis hospitality proverbial and become one of our most distinctive genre institutions, is to strain credulity too far. Are the Colonel's powers of self restraint altogether transcendent? Have we found the living superman at last?

When the Colonel says that he consumed just a part of one he doubtless meant that he did not swallow the Mint itself, munch the ice and devour the very cup.

INTRODUCTION

I have known the author of "The Ideal Bartender" for many years, and it is a genuine privilege to be permitted to testify to his qualifications for such a work.

To his many friends in St. Louis, Louisville, Cincinnati, Chicago and elsewhere, my word will be superfluous, but to those who do not know him, and who are to be the gainers by following his advices, it may prove at the very beginning a stimulus to know something of his record of achievement.

For the past quarter of a century he has refreshed and delighted the members and their friends of the Pendennis Club of Louisville and the St. Louis Country Club of St. Louis. In all that time I doubt if he has erred in even one of his concoctions. Thus if there is "many a slip twixt the cup and the lip" it has been none of his doing, but rather the fault of those who have appreciated his art too highly. But why go on! His work is before you. It is the best to be had. Follow on, and as you sip the nectar of his schemings tell your friends, to the end that both they and he may be benefitted.

G.H. WALKER.

ABRICONTINE POUSSE CAFE

Fill Pousse Cafe glass one-third full of Abricontine and add Maraschino, Curacoa, Chartreuse and Brandy in equal proportions until the glass is filled. The ingredients should be poured in one after the other from a small Wine glass, with great care, to prevent the colors from blending. Ignite the Brandy on top, and after it has blazed for a few seconds extinguishing it by placing a saucer or the bottom of another glass over the blazing fluid. Then serve.

ABSINTHE

(When the customer asks for Absinthe without specifying any particular style of service).

Pour one pony of Absinthe into large Bar glass and let ice cold water drip from the Absinthe glass into Bar glass until full. The Absinthe glass has a hole in the center. By filling the bowl of the Absinthe glass partly with Shaved Ice, and the rest with water, the water will be ice cold as it drops from the Absinthe glass.

ABSINTHE, AMERICAN SERVICE

Mixing glass ¾ full Shaved Ice.

4 dashes Gum Syrup.

1 pony Absinthe.

Shake until outside of shaker is well frosted; strain into large Champagne glass and serve.

ABSINTHE COCKTAIL

Mixing glass ¾ full Shaved Ice.

½ jigger Water.

½ jigger Absinthe.

2 dashes Angostura Bitters.

1 teaspoonful Benedictine.

Stir; strain into Cocktail glass and serve.

ABSINTHE FRAPPE

Fill medium Bar glass full of Shaved Ice.

1 teaspoonful Benedictine.

1 pony Absinthe.

Shake until outside of Shaker has frosty appearance; strain into six-ounce Shell glass and serve.

ABSINTHE, FRENCH SERVICE

Pour 1 pony of Absinthe into a Champagne glass which is standing in a bowl. Fill the bowl of your Absinthe glass with Shaved Ice and water. Raise the bowl and let the Ice Water drip into the Absinthe until the proper color is obtained. Serve in thin Bar glass.

ABSINTHE, ITALIAN SERVICE

1 pony of Absinthe in a large Bar glass.

3 picccs Cracked Ice.

3 dashes Maraschino.

½ pony Anisette.

Pour Ice Water in glass, at same time stirring gently with Bar Spoon. Serve.

ADMIRAL SCHLEY HIGH BALL

Drop a piece of Ice into a High Ball glass.

1 teaspoonful Pineapple Syrup.

1 teaspoonful Lemon Juice.

⅔ jigger Irish Whiskey.

⅔ jigger Tokay, Angelica or Sweet Catawba Wine.

Fill up with Apollinaris or Seltzer.

ALE FLIP

Fill an Ale glass nearly full.

1 teaspoonful of Bar Sugar.

Break in 1 whole Egg; grate a little Nutmeg on top and
serve the drink with a spoon alongside of the glass.

ALE SANGAREE

Dissolve in an Ale glass 1 teaspoonful Bar Sugar. Fill up
with Ale and serve with grated Nutmeg on top.

AMERICAN POUSSE CAFE

Fill a Pousse Cafe glass ¼ full of Chartreuse, and add
Maraschino, Curacoa and Brandy in equal proportions until
the glass is filled. Then proceed as for Abricontine Pousse
Cafe.

APOLLINARIS LEMONADE

Fill large Bar glass ⅔ full Shaved Ice.

2 teaspoonfuls Powdered Sugar.

1 Lemon's Juice.

Fill up with Apollinaris; stir; strain into Lemonade glass
dress with Fruit and serve.

APPLE JACK COCKTAIL

Fill large Bar glass ¾ full Shaved Ice.

3 dashes Gum Syrup.

3 dashes Raspberry Syrup.

1¼ jiggers Applejack.

Shake; strain into Cocktail glass and serve with piece of
Lemon Peel twisted on top.

APPLEJACK FIX

Fill large Bar glass with Shaved Ice.

2 teaspoonfuls Bar Sugar, dissolved in little Water.

¼ Juice of 1 Lemon.

3 dashes of Curacoa.

4 dashes of any Fruit Syrup.

1 jigger Applejack Brandy.

Stir; dress with Fruits; serve with Straws.

APPLEJACK SOUR

Fill large Bar glass ¾ full Shaved Ice.

2 teaspoonfuls Bar Sugar, dissolved in little Water.

3 dashes lemon or Lime Juice.

1 jigger Applejack.

Stir well; strain into Sour glass; dress with Fruit and Berries and serve.

"ARF-AND-ARF"

Pour into an Ale glass or mug ½ Porter and ½ Ale, or Porter and Stout with Ale, or ½ Old and ½ New Ale.

The use of the Porter and Ale is more prevalent in England. In the United States ½ Old and ½ New Ale is usually used when this drink is called for, unless otherwise specified.

ARRACK PUNCH

Pour into a Punch glass the Juice of 1 Lime and a little Apollinaris Water in which a heaping teaspoonful of Bar Sugar has been dissolved. Add:

1 Lump Ice.

¾ jigger Batavia Arrack.

¼ Jigger Jamaica Rum.

Stir well; dash with Champagne; stir again briskly; dress with Fruit and Serve.

ASTRINGENT

½ Wineglass Port Wine.

6 dashes Jamaica Ginger.

Fill up with Brandy; stir gently and serve with little Nutmeg on top.

AUDITORIUM COOLER

Into large Bar glass squeeze Juice of 1 Lemon.

1 teaspoonful Bar Sugar.

1 bottle Ginger Ale off the ice.

Stir; decorate with Fruit and Berries, Serve.

ALL RIGHT COCKTAIL

Use a large Mixing glass filled with Lump Ice.

1 jigger Rye Whiskey.

⅔ jigger Orange Curacoa.

1 dash Angostura Bitters.

Shake well; strain into Cocktail glass and serve.

BACARDI COCKTAIL

Use a large Mixing glass.

Fill with Lump Ice.

½ jigger Cusinier Grenadine.

1 jigger Bacardi Rum.

Shake well and serve in a Cocktail glass.

BACARDI COCKTAIL—Country Club Style

Use a large Mixing glass.

Fill with Lump Ice.

½ Lime Juice.

2 dashes Imported Grenadine.

1 jigger Bacardi Rum.

Shake well; strain into Cocktail glass and serve.

BALDY COCKTAIL

Use a large Mixing glass with Lump Ice.

1 jigger of Burnette's Old Tom Gin.

1 pony of Orange Juice.

1 Dash of Orange Bitters.

Shake; strain into Cocktail glass and serve.

BAMBOO COCKTAIL

Fill large Bar glass ⅓ full Fine Ice.

¾ Sherry Wine.

¾ Italian Vermouth.

Stir; strain into Cocktail glass. Serve.

BLACK COW

Use a large Mixing glass with Lump Ice.

2 jiggers of Cream.

1 bottle Sarsaparilla.

Stir well and serve with Straws.

BLOOD HOUND COCKTAIL

Fill large Bar glass ½ full Shaved Ice.

Add ½ dozen fresh Strawberries.

1 jigger Burnette's Old Tom Gin.

Shake well; strain into Cocktail glass and serve.

BOMBAY COCKTAIL

Use a Claret glass.

½ pony Olive Oil.

½ pony Vinegar.

½ pony Worcestershire Sauce.

Break one Ice Cold Egg into glass.

Add salt and Spanish Paprica and serve.

BENEDICTINE

Place an inverted Whiskey glass on the bar, set a Pony glass on it and fill up with Benedictine. Serve all liquors straight in this manner.

BEEF TEA

½ teaspoonful Beef Extract in small Bar glass.

Fill glass with Hot Water. Stir well while seasoning with Pepper, Salt and Celery Salt. Serve with small glass of Cracked Ice and spoon on the side.

BISHOP

1 teaspoonful Bar Sugar in large Bar glass.

2 dashes Lemon Juice with the Skin of Two Slices.

Fill glass ¾ full Shaved Ice.

1 dash Seltzer Water.

2 dashes Jamaica Rum.

Fill up with Claret or Burgundy; shake; ornament with Fruit and serve with Straws.

BISHOP A LA PRUSSE

Before a Fire or in a Hot Oven roast 6 large Oranges until they are of a light brown color, and then place them in a deep dish and scatter over them ½ lb. of Granulated Sugar and pour on 1 pint of Port or Claret Wine. Then cover the dish and set aside for 24 hours before the time to serve. When about ready for the service, set the dish in boiling water; press the Juice from the Oranges with a large spoon or wooden potato masher and strain the Juice through a fine seive or cheese cloth. Then boil 1 pint of Port or Claret and mix it with the Strained Juice. Serve in stem Claret glasses while warm. A little Nutmeg on top improves the drink, but should not be added unless requested by customer or guest.

BISMARCK

2 teaspoonfuls Vanilla Cordial in Sherry Wine glass.

1 yolk of an Egg covered with Benedictine so as not to
break the yolk.

½ Wineglass Kuemmel.

1 light dash Angostura Bitters.

The colors should be kept separate and great care exercised
to prevent the ingredients from running together.

BIZZY IZZY HIGH BALL

Drop 1 piece of Ice into a Highball glass.

2 dashes Lemon Juice.

2 teaspoonfuls Pineapple Syrup.

½ jigger Sherry Wine.

½ jigger Rye or Bourbon Whiskey.

BLACK STRIPE

Pour Wineglass Santa Cruz or Jamaica Rum into a small
Bar glass and add 1 tablespoonful of Molasses.

If to serve hot, fill glass with boiling Water and sprinkle
Nutmeg on top.

If to serve cold, add ½ Wineglass Water. Stir well and fill
up with Shaved Ice.

BLACK AND TAN PUNCH (For party of 10)

1 lb. white Sugar.

Juice of 6 Lemons.

1 quart Guinness Stout.

1 quart Champagne.

Pour into mixture of Lemon Juice and Sugar the
Champagne and Stout, ice cold. Serve in Punch glasses
dressed with Fruit.

BLACKTHORNE COCKTAIL

Fill Mixing glass ⅔ full Shaved Ice.

¼ teaspoonful Lemon Juice.

1 teaspoonful Syrup.

½ jigger Vermouth.

½ Jigger Sloe Gin.

1 dash Angostura Bitters.

2 dashes Orange Bitters.

Stir; strain into Cocktail glass and serve.

BLACKTHORNE SOUR

Fill large Bar glass ⅔ full Shaved Ice.

4 dashes Lime or Lemon Juice.

1 teaspoonful Pineapple Syrup.

½ teaspoonful green Chartreuse.

1 jigger Sloe Gin.

Stir; strain into Claret glass; ornament with Fruit and serve.

BLIZ'S ROYAL RICKEY

Drop 3 lumps Cracked Ice in a Rickey (thin Champagne) glass.

½ Lime or ¼ Lemon.

4 dashes Raspberry Syrup.

1 pony Vermouth.

¾ jigger Gin.

Fill up with Ginger Ale (imported); stir; dress with Fruit and serve.

BLUE BLAZER

Use two Pewter or Silver Mugs.

1 teaspoonful Bar Sugar dissolved in a little Hot Water.

1 Wineglass (or jigger) Scotch Whiskey.

Ignite the mixture, and while blazing pour it several times from one mug to the other. Serve with a piece of twisted Lemon Peel on top.

BOATING PUNCH

Into a large Bar glass put:

2 teaspoonfuls Bar Sugar.

2 dashes Lemon Juice.

1 dash Lime Juice.

Fill up with Shaved Ice and add:

1 pony Brandy.

1 jigger Santa Cruz Bum.

Stir; dress with Fruit and serve with Straws.

BOMBAY PUNCH (2½-gallon mixture for 40 people)

Bruise the skins of 6 Lemons in 1 lb. of Bar sugar and put
the Sugar in a Punch bowl and add:

1 box Strawberries.

2 Lemons, sliced.

6 Oranges, sliced.

1 Pineapple, cut into small pieces.

1 quart Brandy.

1 quart Sherry Wine.

1 quart Madeira Wine.

Stir well; empty into another bowl in which a block of
Clear Ice has been placed and add:

4 quarts of Champagne.

2 quarts Carbonated Water.

Serve into Punch glasses so that each person will have
some of the Fruit.

BON SOIR ("Good Night")

Fill a Sherry glass ½ full of Shaved Ice.

½ pony Benedictine.

½ pony Creme Yvette.

Fill up with Ginger Ale; stir gently and serve with a Straw
cut in two.

BOSTON COOLER

1 Lemon Rind in large Bar glass. 3 lumps Ice. 1 bottle
Ginger Ale. 1 bottle Sarsaparilla.

Serve.

BOTTLE OF COCKTAIL

Pour a quart of Whiskey or other Liquor desired into a Bar measure or glass pitcher and add:

1 jigger Gum Syrup.

1 pony Curacoa.

¾ pony Angostura Bitters.

Pour back and forth from one measure or pitcher into another measure or pitcher until the liquid is thoroughly mixed. Bottle and cork.

BRACE UP

1 tablespoonful Bar Sugar in large Mixing glass.

3 dashes Boker's or Angostura Bitters.

3 dashes Lemon Juice.

2 dashes Anisette.

1 Egg.

1 jigger Brandy

½ glass Shaved Ice.

Shake well; strain into tall, thin glass; fill with Apollinaris and serve.

BRANDY AND GINGER ALE

3 lumps of Ice in tall, thin glass.

1 Wineglass Brandy.

1 bottle Ginger Ale.

Stir briskly and serve.

BRANDY AND SODA

2 pieces of Ice in tall, thin glass.

1 Wineglass Brandy.

1 bottle plain Soda.

Stir briskly and serve.

BRANDY FLIP

Fill medium. Bar glass ¼ full Shaved Ice.

1 Egg broken in whole.

2 level teaspoonfuls Bar Sugar.

1 jigger Brandy.

Shake well; strain into small Shell glass; grate a little Nutmeg on top and serve.

BRANDY FLOAT

Fill a Cocktail glass ⅔ full of Carbonated Water.

1 pony Brandy floated on top.

(Use spoon to float the Brandy).

BRANDY JULEP

Into a small Bar glass pour ¾ Wineglass of Water and stir in 1 heaping teaspoonful of Bar Sugar. Bruise 3 or 4 sprigs of Mint in the Sugar and Water with a Muddler until the flavor of the Mint has been extracted. Then withdraw the Mint and pour the flavored Water into a tall Shell glass or large Goblet, which has been filled with fine Ice, and add:

1 jigger of Brandy.

2 dashes Jamaica Rum.

Stir well; decorate with few sprigs of Mint by planting the sprigs stems downward in the Ice around the rim of glass; dress with Fruit and serve.

BRANDY PUNCH

Fill large Bar glass ¾ full Shaved Ice.

2 teaspoonfuls Bar Sugar dissolved in little Water.

½ Juice of 1 Lemon.

¼ jigger Santa Cruz Rum.

1½ jiggers Brandy.

1 slice Orange.

1 piece of Pineapple.

Shake; dress with Fruit and serve with Straw.

BRANDY SCAFFA

Into a small Wineglass pour:

Green Chartreuse.

Maraschino.

Old Brandy.

In equal proportion to fill the glass, using care as in
preparing Crustas, not to allow the colors to blend.

BRANDY SHAKE

Fill small Bar glass ¾ full Shaved Ice.

1 teaspoonful Bar Sugar.

Juice of 2 Limes.

1 jigger Brandy.

Shake; strain into small fancy glass and serve.

BRANDY SHRUB (2-gallon mixture for 40 people)

Into a Punch bowl put the Peeled Rinds of 5 Lemons and the Juice of 12 Lemons and add 5 quarts of Brandy. Make the bowl airtight and set it aside. At the expiration of 6 days add 3 quarts of Sherry wine and 6 pounds of Loaf Sugar, which has been dissolved in 1 quart of plain Soda. Strain through a bag and bottle.

BRANDY SKIN

Fill a Whiskey glass ½ full Hot Water and pour in:

1 jigger Brandy.

Twist a piece of Lemon Skin on top and serve.

(It may occur that a customer will ask for a little Sugar. In that case add ½ small teaspoonful, and stir).

BRANDY SLING

In a Whiskey glass:

1 lump Ice.

1 teaspoonful Sugar dissolved in little Water.

1 jigger Brandy.

Stir; twist in a piece of Lemon Peel; grate Nutmeg on top and serve.

BRANDY SMASH

Fill large Bar glass ½ full Shaved Ice.

1 heaping teaspoonful Bar Sugar.

3 sprigs of Mint.

1 jigger Brandy.

Stir; strain into fancy Stem glass and serve.

BRANDY SOUR

Fill large Bar glass ¾ full Shaved Ice.

2 teaspoonfuls Bar Sugar.

3 dashes Lemon or Lime Juice.

3 dashes Seltzer or Apollinaris Water.

1 jigger Brandy.

Stir; strain into Sour glass; dress with Fruit and serve.

BRANDY TODDY

Into a Whiskey glass drop 1 lump Cracked Ice.

1 teaspoonful of Bar Sugar dissolved in little Water.

Stir; place the bottle before the customer and allow him to pour his own drink.

BRONX COCKTAIL

Fill large Bar glass ¾ full Shaved Ice.

⅓ jigger Dry Gin.

⅓ jigger French Vermouth.

⅓ jigger Italian Vermouth.

1 Slice Orange.

Shake well; strain into Cocktail glass and serve.

BURNT BRANDY

Place two lumps of Cut Loaf Sugar in a small, shallow dish or saucer and pour over the Sugar 1½ jiggers of Cognac Brandy. Ignite the Sugar and Brandy and let them burn for about two minutes. Then cover the dish or saucer with a plate, and when the fire is extinguished pour the liquid into a small Bar glass and serve.

BUSTER BROWN COCKTAIL

Fill large Bar glass ⅔ full Shaved Ice.

1 teaspoonful Gum Syrup.

2 dashes Lemon Juice.

2 dashes Orange Bitters.

1 jigger Whiskey.

Stir; strain into Cocktail glass and serve.

BUTTERED RUM

In a Tumbler drop 1 lump of Sugar and dissolve it in a little hot Water, and add:

1¼ Jiggers Rum.

1 piece of Butter about the size of a Walnut.

Grate Nutmeg on top and serve.

CALIFORNIA SHERRY COBBLER

1 pony of Pineapple Syrup in large Bar glass.

2 jiggers California Sherry.

Fill glass with Shaved Ice; stir well; decorate with Fruit; dash a little Port Wine on top and serve with Straws.

CALIFORNIA WINE COBBLER

Fill tall, thin glass nearly full Shaved Ice.

1 heaping teaspoonful Bar Sugar.

Juice of 1 Orange.

2½ jiggers California Wine.

Stir; ornament with Fruit and serve with Straws.

CARLETON RICKEY—St. Louis Style

Use a large Mixing glass; fill with lump Ice.

Juice 1 Lime.

Drop squeezed Lime in glass.

1 jigger Old Bourbon Whiskey.

Fill with Sweet Soda.

Stir well and serve.

CATAWBA COBBLER

Fill large Bar glass ½ full of Shaved Ice.

1 teaspoonful Bar Sugar dissolved in a little Water.

1½ jiggers Catawba Wine.

¼ slice of Orange.

Fill with Shaved Ice; stir well; decorate with Berries and serve with Straws.

CELERY SOUR

Fill large Bar glass full Shaved Ice.

1 teaspoonful Lemon Juice.

1 teaspoonful Pineapple Syrup.

1 teaspoonful Celery Bitters.

Stir; strain into Fancy Wineglass with Fruit and serve.

CENTURY CLUB PUNCH (for a party of 5)

Fill glass Pitcher ¼ full Cracked Ice.

½ pint Jamaica Rum.

½ pint Santa Cruz Rum.

2½ pints aerated Water.

2½ tablespoonfuls Bar Sugar.

Stir well and serve in Punch glasses.

CHAMPAGNE

Serve off the Ice very cold. Ice should never be put in the Wine.

CHAMPAGNE COBBLER

1 teaspoonful Bar Sugar in large Bar glass.

1 slice Lemon Peel.

1 slice Orange Peel

Fill glass ½ full Shaved Ice and fill up with Champagne. Decorate with Fruit and serve with Straws.

CHAMPAGNE COCKTAIL

1 lump Sugar in tall, thin glass.

1 small piece Ice.

2 dashes Angostura Bitters.

1 piece twisted Lemon Peel.

Fill up with Champagne.

Stir and serve.

CHAMPAGNE CUP (2-gallon mixture)

For mixing use a large Punch bowl or other suitable vessel of glass or porcelain lined.

4 Oranges, sliced.

4 Lemons, sliced.

½ Pineapple, sliced.

½ pint Chartreuse.

½ pint Abricontine.

1 pint Curacoa.

1 pint Cognac Brandy.

1 pint Tokay Wine.

Stir well and allow mixture to stand three hours. Strain into another bowl and add:

3 quarts Champagne.

3 pints Apollinaris Water.

1 large piece of Ice.

Stir well; decorate with Fruit; float slices of Grape Fruit on top and serve in Champagne glasses.

CHAMPAGNE FRAPPE

Place a bottle in a Champagne cooler and around it a freezing mixture of fine Ice and Salt. Twirl the bottle until it is about to freeze, when it will be ready to serve.

CHAMPAGNE JULEP

Fill medium size Shell glass ⅓ full Cracked Ice.

2 teaspoonfuls Bar Sugar.

2 sprigs bruised Mint.

Pour Champagne slowly into the glass, stirring gently at the same time.

Dress with fruit; dash with Brandy and serve with Straws.

CHAMPAGNE PUNCH (for a party of 6)

Into a glass Pitcher pour the Juice of 1 Lemon, and add:

¼ lb. Bar Sugar.

1 jigger Strawberry Syrup.

1 quart bottle Champagne.

Stir with Ladle and drop in:

1 sliced Orange.

3 slices Pineapple.

Decorate with Fruit and serve in Champagne goblets.

CHAMPAGNE SOUR

Fill medium Bar glass ⅓ full Shaved Ice.

3 dashes Lemon Juice.

Fill up with Champagne.

Stir gently; dress with Fruit and Berries; dash with Brandy
and serve with Straws.

CHAMPAGNE VELVET

Fill Goblet ½ full ice-cold Champagne. Fill up balance of Goblet with ice-cold Porter. Stir and serve.

CHOCOLATE PUNCH

Fill large Bar glass ⅔ full Shaved Ice.

1 teaspoonful Bar Sugar.

¼ jigger Curacoa.

1 jigger Port Wine.

1 Egg.

Fill up with Milk; shake well; strain into Punch glass; grate Nutmeg on top and serve.

CIDER EGGNOG

Into a large Bar glass break a fresh Egg.

1 teaspoonful Sugar.

4 lumps Cracked Ice.

Fill up with Sweet Cider.

Shake; strain into tall, thin glass and serve with grated
Nutmeg on top.

CLARET AND ICE

4 lumps Ice in medium size Mineral Water glass.

Fill up with Claret and serve.

CLARET COBBLER

Dissolve one teaspoonful of Sugar with little Water in large Bar glass.

1 quartered slice Orange.

2 jiggers Claret.

Fill up with Shaved Ice and serve with Straws.

CLARET CUP (2-gallon mixture)

For mixing use a large Punch bowl or other suitable vessel of glass or porcelain lined.

6 Oranges, sliced.

3 Lemons, sliced.

2 Pineapples.

2 jiggers Abricontine.

4 jiggers Curacoa.

4 quarts Claret.

3 pints Apollinaris.

Mix well with a Ladle and set aside for three hours before using. Then strain info another bowl, and when ready to use add 3 pints of some sparkling Wine, preferably Champagne. Stir gently once or twice, and then put in a block of clear Ice and decorate the top of it tastily with Fruits and let several slices of Grape Fruit float around in the bowl. Serve in Champagne glasses.

CLARET FLIP

Fill large Bar glass ½ full Shaved Ice.

2 heaping teaspoonfuls Bar Sugar dissolved in a little Water.

1 whole Egg broken in.

1½ Jiggers Claret Wine.

Shake thoroughly; strain into Punch glass; sprinkle with Nutmeg on top and serve.

CLARET PUNCH

Fill large Bar glass ⅔ full Shaved Ice.

3 teaspoonfuls Bar Sugar.

4 dashes Lemon Juice.

2 slices Orange.

2 jiggers Claret.

Shake; strain into thin glass; dress with Fruit and serve with Straws.

CLARET PUNCH (5-gallon mixture for a large reception or party of 100 people)

For mixing use a large agate or porcelain-lined vessel.

4 lbs. Cut Loaf Sugar.

Juice of 25 Lemons.

2 quarts Brandy.

10 quarts Claret.

7 jiggers Chartreuse (green).

8 quarts Carbonated Water.

Stir well.

Place a large block of Ice in a Punch bowl and fill nearly full of the mixture, adding:

18 Oranges, cut in slices.

1½ cans sliced Pineapples.

Serve from the bowl into Punch glasses with a Ladle, and renew the contents of the bowl from the mixing vessel as needed.

CLOVER CLUB COCKTAIL

Fill large Bar glass ½ full Fine Ice.

½ pony Raspberry Syrup.

½ jigger Dry Gin.

½ jigger French Vermouth.

White of 1 Egg.

Shake well; strain into Cocktail glass and serve.

CLOVER LEAF COCKTAIL

Fill Mixing glass with Lump Ice.

½ pony Cusenier Grenadine.

The white of one Egg.

1 jigger Sir Robert Burnette's Old Tom Gin.

Shake well and strain into a Cocktail glass.

CLUB COCKTAIL

Fill large Bar glass ½ full Shaved Ice.

2 dashes Angostura Bitters.

2 dashes Pineapple Syrup.

1 jigger Brandy.

Stir; strain into Cocktail glass; dress with Berries; dash with Champagne; twist a piece of Lemon Skin over the drink and drop it on top. Serve.

CLUB HOUSE CLARET PUNCH

Fill large Bar glass ¾ full Shaved Ice.

4 dashes Gum Syrup.

1 teaspoonful Lemon Juice.

1 teaspoonful Orange Juice.

2 jiggers Claret.

Shake; strain into tall, thin glass; fill up with Apollinaris or Seltzer; dress with Fruit and serve.

CLUB HOUSE PUNCH (for a party of 20)

For mixing use a large Punch bowl.

½ can Peaches.

½ can Pineapples.

3 Oranges, sliced.

3 Lemons, sliced.

3 quarts Sweet Catawba or Tokay.

1 pint Brandy.

1½ jiggers Jamaica Rum.

1 jigger Green Chartreuse.

Set this mixture aside in ice box for 6 hours. Then place block of Ice in another bowl of sufficient capacity and strain in the mixture from the Mixing bowl. Dress the Ice with Fruit and serve with a Ladle into Punch glasses.

COFFEE COCKTAIL

Fill large Bar glass ⅔ full Shaved Ice.

1 fresh Egg.

1 teaspoonful Bar Sugar.

1 jigger Port Wine.

1 pony Brandy.

Shake; strain into medium thin glass; grate Nutmeg on top and serve.

COHASSET PUNCH

Fill large Bar glass ½ full Shaved Ice.

1 jigger New England Rum.

1 jigger Vermouth.

3 dashes Gum Syrup.

1 dash Orange Bitters.

½ juice of a Lemon

Stir and serve with a Preserved Peach and its liquor.

COLD RUBY PUNCH (2½-gallon mixture for 50 people)

4 lbs. Cut Loaf Sugar.

2 quarts Port Wine.

2 quarts Batavia Arrack.

6 quarts green Tea.

Juice of 24 Lemons.

(See instructions for mixing and serving Punches in quantities.)

COLUMBIA SKIN

This drink is identical with Whiskey Skin.

COMPANION PUNCH (2½-gallon mixture for a reception or party of 50 people)

Into a large Punch bowl pour:

1¼ pints Lemon Juice.

2 pints Gum Syrup.

¾ pint Orange Juice.

1¼ pints Brandy.

6 quarts equal parts Sweet and Dry Catawba.

2 quarts Carbonated Water.

When well stirred place large block of Ice in center of bowl; dress the Ice with Fruit and serve with a Ladle into Punch glasses.

CONTINENTAL SOUR

Fill a large Bar glass ⅔ full Shaved Ice.

1 teaspoonful Bar Sugar dissolved in little Water.

Juice of ½ Lemon.

1 jigger of Whiskey, Brandy or Gin, as preferred.

Shake; strain into Sour glass; dash with Claret and serve.

CORDIAL LEMONADE

Add to a plain Lemonade ⅓ Jigger of any Cordial which the customer may prefer, and serve.

COUNTRY COCKTAIL

Fill large Bar glass ⅔ full Shaved Ice.

1 teaspoonful Bar Sugar.

1 pony Brandy.

1 jigger Port Wine.

1 Egg.

Shake well; strain into thin glass; grate Nutmeg on top and serve.

COUPEREE

Fill large Bar glass ⅓ full Ice Cream.

¾ jigger Brandy.

1 pony Bed Curacoa.

Mix thoroughly with a spoon.

Fill up with Plain Soda; grate Nutmeg on top and serve.

CREME DE MENTHE

Fill a Sherry glass with Shaved Ice.

1 pony Creme de Menthe.

Cut Straw in two pieces and serve.

CRIMEAN CUP A LA MARMORA (for a party of 10)

Into a small Punch bowl pour:

1 pint Orgeat Syrup.

2 jiggers Jamaica Rum.

2 jiggers Maraschino.

2½ jiggers Brandy.

2 tablespoonfuls Bar Sugar.

1 quart Champagne.

1 quart Plain Soda.

Stir well; pack the bowl in Fine Ice, and when cold serve in fancy Stem glasses.

COUNTRY CLUB PUNCH

Take 1½ lbs. of Cut Loaf Sugar and rub the lumps on the skins of 4 Lemons and 2 Oranges until the Sugar becomes well saturated with the oil from the skins. Then put the Sugar thus prepared into a large porcelain-lined or agate Mixing vessel, and add:

12 Oranges, sliced.

1 Pineapple, sliced.

1 box Strawberries.

2 bottles (quarts) Apollinaris Water.

Stir thoroughly with oak paddle or large silver ladle, and add:

1 jigger Benedictine.

1 jigger Red Curacoa.

1 jigger Maraschino.

½ jigger Jamaica Rum.

1 quart Brandy.

4 quarts Tokay or Sweet Catawba Wine.

2 quarts Madeira Wine.

4 quarts Chateau Margaux.

Mix well with oak paddle or ladle and strain into another bowl in which has been placed a block of clear ice. Then pour in 6 quarts Champagne. Decorate the Ice with Fruits, Berries, etc. Serve in Punch cups or glasses, dressing each glass with Fruit and Berries from the bowl.

COOPERSTOWN COCKTAIL

Use a large Bar glass.

Fill with Lump Ice.

One jigger of Sir Robert Burnette's Old Tom Gin.

½ pony of Italian Vermouth.

Six leaves of fresh Mint.

Shake ingredients well together.

Strain and serve in Cocktail glass.

CURACOA

Into a bottle which will hold a full quart, or a little over, drop 6 ounces of Orange Peel sliced very thin, and add 1 pint of Whiskey. Cork the bottle securely and let it stand two weeks, shaking the bottle frequently during that time. Next strain, the mixture, add the Syrup, pour the strained mixture back into the cleaned bottle and let it stand 3 days, shaking well now and then during the first day. Next, pour a teacupful of the mixture into a mortar and beat up with it 1 drachm Powdered Alum, 1 drachm Carbonate of Potash. Put this mixture back into the bottle and let it stand for 10 days, at the expiration of which time the Curacoa will be clear and ready for use.

CURACOA PUNCH

Fill large Bar glass ¾ full Shaved Ice.

2 teaspoonfuls Bar Sugar.

4 dashes Lemon Juice.

1 pony Red Curacoa.

1 jigger Brandy.

½ pony Jamaica Rum.

Stir; decorate with Fruit and Serve with Straws.

CURRANT SHRUB

For mixing use a porcelain-lined or agate vessel, and put in:

1½ lbs. Cut Loaf Sugar.

1 quart Currant Juice

Place vessel on the fire and let it boil slowly for 10 minutes, and skim well while boiling. Then remove vessel from fire and add ½ gill of Brandy to every pint of Shrub. Bottle and cork securely. This drink is served by simply pouring a little of the Syrup into Ice Water, as any drink from Fruit Syrup is prepared. The basis preparation for all Shrubs or Small Fruits, such as Cherries, Raspberries, etc., is prepared in the same way as directed for Currant Shrub, varying the quantity of Sugar used to suit the kind of Fruit.

DERONDA COCKTAIL

Fill large Bar glass with Shaved Ice.

1½ jiggers Calisaya.

1½ jiggers Plymouth Gin.

Shake; strain into Cocktail glass and serve.

DIARRHEA DRAUGHT

Into a Whiskey glass pour:

½ jigger Blackberry Brandy.

½ pony Peach Brandy.

2 dashes Jamaica Ginger.

Grate Nutmeg on top and serve.

DIXIE COCKTAIL

Add to a plain Whiskey Cocktail:

1 dash Curacoa.

6 drops Creme de Menthe.

DREAM

Fill large Bar glass ⅔ full Shaved Ice.

1 teaspoonful Bar Sugar.

3 dashes Lemon Juice.

1 white of an Egg.

1 Wineglass Milk and Cream.

1 jigger Tom Gin.

Shake thoroughly; strain into tall, thin glass; cover the top lightly with Creme de Menthe and serve.

DELUSION

Use a large Mixing glass; fill with Shaved Ice.

½ Lime Juice.

⅔ white Creme de Menthe.

⅓ Apricot Brandy.

Shake well; strain into thin Stem glass and serve.

DORAY PUNCH

Fill large Bar glass ⅔ full Shaved Ice.

2 teaspoonfuls Lemon Juice.

4 dashes Pineapple Syrup.

4 dashes Gum Syrup.

¼ jigger Jamaica Rum.

¼ jigger green Chartreuse.

½ jigger Tokay Wine.

½ jigger Brandy.

1 white of an Egg.

Shake hard; strain into thin Bar glass; dress with Fruit; dash with Seltzer; grate Nutmeg on top and serve.

DORAY SOUR

Fill large Bar glass ⅔ full Shaved Ice.

3 dashes Gum Syrup

4 dashes Lemon Juice.

1 dash Lime Juice.

1 teaspoonful Abricontine or green Chartreuse.

½ jigger Tokay or Sweet Catawba Wine.

½ jigger Brandy.

Stir well and strain into a fancy Sour glass; dress with Fruits; dash with Apollinaris or Seltzer; top off with a little Claret and serve.

DUPLEX COCKTAIL

Fill large Bar glass with Shaved Ice.

⅓ Jigger Old Tom Gin.

1 pony Italian Vermouth.

1 pony French Vermouth.

3 dashes Acid Phosphate.

4 dashes Orange Bitters.

Shake; strain into Cocktail glass and serve.

DURKEE COCKTAIL

Fill large Bar glass ⅔ Full Shaved Ice.

1 tablespoonful Bar Sugar.

4 dashes Lemon Juice.

3 dashes Curacoa.

1 jigger Jamaica Rum.

Shake well; strain into tall, thin glass; fill up with Plain
Soda; stir gently and serve.

EAGLE PUNCH

Into a Hot Water glass drop:

1 lump Cut Loaf Sugar and dissolve in little Hot Water, crashing with muddler.

½ jigger Bourbon Whiskey.

½ jigger Rye Whiskey.

Fill up with boiling Water; twist a piece of Lemon Peel and grate Nutmeg on top and serve.

EAST INDIA COCKTAIL

Fill large Bar glass ¾ full Shaved Ice.

3 dashes Maraschino.

3 dashes Red Curacoa.

3 dashes Angostura Bitters.

1 jigger Brandy.

Stir well; strain into Cocktail glass and serve with a piece of twisted Lemon Peel on top.

EGG MILK PUNCH

Fill large Bar glass ½ full Shaved Ice.

2 teaspoonfuls Bar Sugar.

1 Egg

1 pony Santa Cruz Rum.

1 jigger Brandy.

Fill up with Milk; shake thoroughly until the mixture creams; strain into tall thin glass; grate Nutmeg on top and serve.

EGGNOG

Fill large Bar glass ½ full Shaved Ice.

1 Egg

1 teaspoonful Bar Sugar.

¾ jigger Brandy.

½ jigger Jamaica Rum.

Fill up with Milk; shake thoroughly; strain into tall, thin glass and serve with little Nutmeg grated on top.

EGGNOG (bowl of 3 gallons)

Beat the yolks of 20 Eggs until thin and stir in 2½ lbs. Bar Sugar until Sugar is thoroughly dissolved. Into this mixture pour:

1½ pints Jamaica Rum.

2 quarts old Brandy.

Mix the ingredients well by stirring. Then pour in the milk slowly, stirring all the while to prevent curdling. Pour carefully over the top of the mixture the whites of the Eggs, which have been beaten to a stiff froth. Fill Punch glasses from the bowl with ladle and sprinkle a little Nutmeg over each glassful.

EGG SOUR

Into small Bar glass drop:

3 lumps Ice.

1 tablespoonful Bar Sugar.

1 Egg.

Juice of 1 Lemon.

Shake well; grate Nutmeg on top and serve with Straw.

EL DORADO PUNCH

Fill large Bar glass nearly full Shaved Ice.

1 tablespoonful Bar Sugar.

¼ jigger Whiskey.

¼ jigger Jamaica Rum.

½ jigger Brandy.

1 slice Lemon.

Shake; dress with Fruit and serve with Straws.

ENGLISH BISHOP PUNCH

Roast an Orange before a fire or in a hot oven. When brown cut it in quarters and drop the pieces, with a few Cloves, into a small porcelain-lined or agate vessel, and pour in 1 quart of hot Port Wine. Add 6 lumps Cut Loaf Sugar and let the mixture simmer over the fire for 30 minutes. Serve in Stem glasses with Nutmeg grated on top.

FANCY WHISKEY SMASH

Fill large Bar glass ½ full Shaved Ice.

2 teaspoonfuls Bar Sugar.

3 sprigs Mint pressed with muddler in 1 jigger aerated
Water.

1 jigger Whiskey.

Stir well; strain into Sour glass; dress with Fruit and serve.

FANNIE WARD

Use a large Mixing glass with Lump Ice.

White of an Egg.

Juice ½ Lime.

2 dashes imported Grenadine.

1 jigger Bacardi Rum.

Shake and strain into Cocktail glass.

FEDORA

Fill large Bar glass ¾ full Shaved Ice.

2 teaspoonfuls Bar Sugar dissolved in little Water.

1 pony Curacoa.

1 pony Brandy.

½ pony Jamaica Hum.

½ pony Whiskey.

Shake well; dress with Fruit and serve with Straws.

FISH CLUB PUNCH (for a party of 8)

Into a Punch bowl pour:

2½ jiggers Lemon Juice.

4 jiggers Peach Brandy.

2 jiggers Cognac Brandy.

2 jiggers Jamaica Rum.

3 pints Ice Water.

Stir well; ladle into Punch glass and serve.

FOG HORN—Country Club Style

Use a large Mixing glass; fill with Lump Ice.

½ Lime Juice.

½ Lemon Juice.

1 teaspoonful Bar Sugar.

1 jigger Burnette's Old Tom Gin.

Stir well; strain into tall, thin glass and fill with imported Ginger Ale.

FREE LOVE COCKTAIL—-Club Style

Lump Ice.

Use Shaker.

½ of the white of 1 Egg.

3 dashes Anisette.

1 jigger Old Tom Gin.

1 pony fresh Cream.

Shake well, serve in Cocktail glass.

FRENCH POUSSE CAFE

Fill a Pousse Cafe glass ½ full of Maraschino and add:
Raspberry Syrup, Vanilla, Curacoa, Chartreuse and Brandy
in equal proportions until the glass is filled. Then proceed
as for Abricontine Pousse Cafe.

GARDEN PUNCH (2½ gallon mixture for a party of 50)

Place a good size block of Ice in a large Punch bowl.

4 jiggers Lemon Juice.

1½ lbs. Bar Sugar.

2 jiggers Orange Juice.

1½ jiggers green Chartreuse.

1 quart Brandy.

6 Quarts Tokay or Sweet Catawba Wine.

2 quarts Claret Wine.

Stir well; ladle into Stem glasses, and decorate each glass
with Fruit before serving.

G.O.P.

Use a large Mixing glass with Lump of Ice.

2 jiggers of Orange Juice.

2 jiggers of Grape Fruit Juice.

Fill with Seltzer Water.

Stir; ornament with Fruit and serve with Straws.

GIBSON COCKTAIL

Use a large Mixing glass with Lump Ice.

1 jigger Gordon Gin.

1 pony French Vermouth.

Stir; strain and serve in Cocktail glass.

GILLETTE COCKTAIL—Chicago Style

Use a large Mixing glass; fill with Lump Ice.

Juice ½ Lime.

1½ jiggers Burnette's Old Tom Gin.

½ teaspoonful Bar Sugar.

Stir well and strain into Cocktail glass.

GIN AND CALAMUS

Put ½ oz. of Calamus Root, which has been steeped, into a quart bottle of Gin.

Serve as you would a Straight Drink.

GIN DAISY

Juice of ½ of a Lime.

1 pony Cusenier Grenadine.

1 jigger Sir Robert Burnette's Old Tom Gin.

Serve in a Mug with Lump Ice; fill with Seltzer.

Stir well and decorate with the skin of the Lime and fresh
Mint and serve with Straws.

GIN SOUR—Country Club Style

Use a large Mixing glass.

Fill with Lump Ice.

½ Lime Juice.

½ Orange Juice.

2 dashes Pineapple Juice.

½ pony Rock Candy Syrup.

1 jigger Burnette's Old Tom Gin.

Shake well; strain into Cocktail glass and serve.

GIN SQUASH—Country Club Style

Use a large glass Stein; fill with Lump Ice.

1 pony Lemon Juice.

1 jigger Orange Juice.

1 pony Pineapple Juice.

1 pony Rock Candy Syrup.

1 jigger Burnette's Old Tom Gin.

Fill with Seltzer: stir well and serve.

GOLFER'S DELIGHT—Home of Bevo—18th Hole.

Use a large glass Pitcher; fill with Lump Ice.

2 bottles Bevo.

2 bottles Sweet Soda.

Stir well and serve in a Beer glass.

Fifty-fifty.

HORSE THIEF COCKTAIL

Fill a large Mixing glass with Lump Ice.

2 dashes green Absinthe.

½ pony Italian Vermouth.

1 jigger Sir Robert Burnette's Old Tom Gin.

Stir well and serve in a Cocktail glass.

IRISH ROSE—Country Club Style

Use a tall, thin glass; fill with Cracked Ice.

1 pony imported Grenadine.

1 jigger Old Bushmill Whiskey.

Fill with Seltzer.

Stir well and serve.

JERSEY LIGHTNING COCKTAIL

Use large Mixing glass; fill with Lump Ice.

1 jigger Apple Jack Brandy.

1 pony Italian Vermouth.

Stir well; strain and serve in Cocktail glass.

KNABENSCHUE—Country Club Style

Use a small stone Mug; Lump Ice.

1 lump Sugar.

2 dashes Angostura Bitters.

Fill with Champagne.

Stir well; dress with fresh Mint and serve.

L.P.W.

Use a large Mixing glass.

Fill with Lump See.

1 jigger of Sir Robert Burnette's Old Tom Gin.

½ pony of Italian Vermouth.

½ pony of French Vermouth.

Stir well and strain into a Cocktail glass.

Add a Pickeled Onion and serve.

LADIES' DELIGHT—Thursday Luncheon Punch

1 quart of Orange Pekoe Tea (cold).

1 quart of Old Country Club Brandy.

1 pint of Lemon Juice.

1 pint of Orange Juice.

½ pint of Pineapple Juice.

2 quarts Berncastler Berg.

1 pint of Bar Sugar.

Use a large Punch bowl with one Lump of Ice.

Pour in mixture; add one quart of Cook's Imperial Champagne.

Stir well; decorate with fresh Mint, Fruit in season, and serve.

LEAPING FROG

1 jigger Hungarian Apricot Brandy.

Juice of ½ Lime.

Fill glass with Lump Ice.

Shake well and strain into Stem glass.

LEMONADE APOLLINARIS (or Carbonated Water)

Fill large Mixing glass ⅔ full fine Ice.

1 tablespoonful Bar Sugar.

Juice of 1 Lemon.

Fill up with Apollinaris or suitable Carbonated Water. Stir; strain into Lemonade glass; dress with Fruit and serve.

LONE TREE COCKTAIL

Use a large Mixing glass; fill with Lump Ice.

1 jigger Burnette's Old Tom Gin.

⅓ Italian Vermouth.

⅓ French Vermouth.

Shake well; serve in Cocktail glass.

MINT JULEP—Kentucky Style

Use a large Silver Mug.

Dissolve one lump of Sugar in one-half pony of Water.

Fill mug with Fine Ice.

Two jiggers of Old Bourbon Whiskey.

Stir well; add one boquet of Mint and serve.

Be careful and not bruise the Mint.

OVERALL JULEP—St. Louis Style

Use a large Mixing glass; fill with Lump Ice.

⅔ Wineglass Rye Whiskey.

⅔ Wineglass Gordon Gin.

½ Wineglass Imported Grenadine.

Juice ½ Lemon.

Juice ½ Lime.

Shake well; pour into tall, thin glass; add one bottle
Imported Club Soda and serve.

ONION COCKTAIL

1 jigger of Burnette's Tom Gin.

½ of Italian Vermouth and no Bitters used.

Large Bar glass with Cracked Ice and stir well.

Strain and serve with an Onion.

OLD FASHION COCKTAIL

Use a Toddy glass.

1 lump of Ice.

2 dashes of Angostura Bitters.

1 lump of Sugar and dissolve in Water.

1½ jiggers of Bourbon Whiskey.

Twist piece of Lemon Skin over the drink and drop it in.
Stir well and serve.

OJEN COCKTAIL

Use an old-fashion Toddy glass.

1 lump Ice.

Juice of ½ of a Lime.

1 dash Angostura Bitters.

2 dashes of Seltzer Water.

Stir well and serve.

PEQUOT SEMER

Use a tall, thin Bar glass.

Juice of a Lime.

Three sprigs of fresh Mint.

1 dash Cusenier Grenadine.

½ pony Pineapple Juice.

½ pony Orange Juice.

1 jigger of Sir Robert Burnette's Old Tom Gin.

Crush ingredients together; fill with Lump Ice; add Seltzer.
Stir well and serve.

PINEAPPLE JULEP (for a party of 6—Use a small punch bowl)

1 quart of Sparkling Moselle.

1 jigger Cusenier Grenadine.

1 jigger Maraschino.

1 jigger Sir Robert Burnette's Old Tom Gin.

1 jigger Lemon Juice.

1 jigger Orange Bitters.

1 jigger Angostura Bitters.

4 Oranges, sliced.

2 Lemons, sliced.

1 ripe Pineapple, sliced and quartered.

4 tablespoonfuls Sugar.

1 bottle Apollinaris Water.

Place large square of Ice in bowl; dress with the Fruits and serve Julep in fancy Stem glass.

POLO PLAYERS' DELIGHT—Horse's Neck

Use a tall, thin glass.

1 lump Ice.

1 jigger Sir Robert Burnette's Old Tom Gin.

1 Cantrell & Cochran's Ginger Ale.

Stir well and serve.

POUSSE CAFE—St. Louis

Pour in Pousse Cafe glass as follows:

⅙ glass Raspberry Syrup.

⅙ glass Maraschino.

⅙ glass Green Vanilla.

⅙ glass Curacao.

⅙ glass Yellow Chartreuse.

⅙ glass Brandy.

In preparing the above use a small Wineglass with spoon for pouring in each Cordial separately.

Be careful they do not mix together.

PUNCH A LA ROMAINE (for a party of 16)

1 bottle Champagne.

1 bottle Rum.

2 tablespoons Dr. Siegert's genuine Angostura Bitters.

10 Lemons.

3 sweet Oranges.

2 pounds Powdered Sugar.

10 fresh Eggs.

Dissolve the Sugar in the Juice of the Lemons and Oranges adding the Rind of 1 Orange.

Strain through a Sieve into a bowl and add by degrees the whites of the Eggs beaten to a froth.

Place the bowl on Ice till cold, then stir in the Rum and Wine until thoroughly mixed. Serve in fancy Stem glasses.

RAMOS GIN FIZZ—Country Club Style

1 lump Ice.

1 dash Lemon Juice.

1 dash Orange Water.

White of Egg.

1 jigger Burnette's Old Tom Gin.

1 teaspoonful Powdered Sugar.

1 pony Milk.

1 dash Seltzer Water.

Shake well; strain into Highball glass and serve.

REMSEN COOLER

Use a medium size Fizz glass.

Peel a Lemon as you would an Apple.

Place the Rind or Peeling into the Fizz glass.

2 or 3 lumps of Crystal Ice.

1 Wineglass of Remsen Scotch Whiskey.

Fill up the balance with Club Soda; stir up slowly with a spoon and serve.

In this country it is often the ease that people call a Remsen Cooler where they want Old Tom Gin or Sloe Gin instead of Scotch Whiskey. It is therefore the bartender's duty to mix as desired.

SEPTEMBER MORN COCKTAIL—Country Club Style

Use a large Mixing glass; fill with Lump Ice.

½ Lime Juice.

1 jigger Burnette's Old Tom Gin.

2 dashes Imported Grenadine.

Shake well; strain into Cocktail glass and serve.

SHANDY GAFF

Use a large Bar glass.

Fill half the glass with Porter and half with Ginger Ale. It is also made with half Ale and half Ginger Ale.

SHERRY AND BITTERS

Put 2 dashes Dr. Siegert's genuine Angostura Bitters in a Sherry glass and roil the glass 'till the Bitters entirely cover the inside surface.

Fill the glass with Sherry and serve.

STINGER—Country Club Style

Use a large Mixing glass; fill with Lump Ice.

1 jigger Old Brandy.

1 pony white Creme de Menthe.

Shake well; strain into Cocktail glass and serve.

STONE SOUR

Use a tall, thin glass; fill with fine Ice.

½ pony Lemon Juice.

½ pony Orange Juice.

2 dashes Rock Candy Syrup.

1 jigger Old Tom Gin.

Leave in Ice; stir well and serve.

SAMTON COCKTAIL

Use a large Mixing glass with Cracked Ice.

1 jigger Orange Juice.

1 jigger imported Ginger Ale.

Fifty-fifty.

Shake well; strain into Cocktail glass and serve.

TOM TOM

Use a large Brandy Roller glass.

Fill Roller half full of Fine Ice.

Add 1 pony of Old Brandy.

1 jigger of green Creme de Menthe and serve.

TOM AND JERRY

Make a batter by separating the yolks from whites of a given number of Eggs; beating the whites to a stiff froth and stirring the yolks until very thin. Then mix together in a Tom and Jerry bowl, stirring in Bar Sugar slowly until the batter is stiff and serve as follows:

Fill Tom and Jerry Mug ¼ full of Batter.

½ jigger Rum.

½ jigger Brandy.

Stir well with Bar spoon; fill up with Hot Water; stir more; grate Nutmeg on top and serve.

TOKAY PUNCH

Out of 6 pounds of Tokay Grapes, select one pound to be put into the Punch last. Now make a boiling Syrup of three pounds of Sugar and one quart of boiling Water and pour this over the remaining five pounds of Grapes. When partly cold rub it through a sieve, leaving skins and seeds behind. Then add the Juice of two Oranges and two Lemons and one quart of St. Julien Claret, 1 jigger of Angostura Bitters.

Then strain and freeze.

Before serving add 1 pint of good Brandy and an Italian Meringue Paste of six Egg whites, colored a nice red and drop in the remaining Grapes.

TWILIGHT COCKTAIL

Use a large Mixing glass with Lump Ice.

1 jigger Bourbon.

½ pony Italian Vermouth.

Juice of whole Lime.

Shake well; strain into a Champagne glass; fill with Seltzer and serve.

WHISKEY PUNCH—St. Louis Style

Use a large Mixing glass; fill with Lump Ice.

One jigger Bourbon Whiskey.

½ pony Italian Vermouth.

½ pony Pineapple Syrup.

½ pony Lemon Juice.

Shake well; strain into Stem glass and serve.

WHISKEY SCOTCH HOT

1 lump Sugar dissolved in Hot Whiskey glass.

1 jigger Scotch Whiskey.

Fill up with Hot Water.

1 slice Lemon Peel.

Stir and serve with Nutmeg sprinkled on top.

WHISKEY IRISH HOT

Substitute Irish for Scotch Whiskey and proceed as for Hot Scotch Whiskey.

Made in the USA
Columbia, SC
23 February 2022

56660793R00059